BETH SEILONEN

RAVYNESS DRAKON
TAROT

REDFeather™
MIND | BODY | SPIRIT

To the dragons who have flown into my life and encouraged me to be the best possible version of myself, to continue to grow, and to fly into a most incredible life, this book is dedicated to you.
Thank you for being a part of my life and my world.

CONTENTS

The story of this deck began when I decided to do something I had always dreamt of. I took myself out to learn and enjoy an evening of ballroom dancing.

I was particularly drawn to one dancer. He moved with ease and gentle confidence. It made one feel comfortable and safe, and he became an instant friend. Over time I found that I had befriended a man who modeled how to be secure in one's emotions, to vocalize needs and desires, to develop personal identity through passions, and to manifest a healthier life style.

He had been working towards his own life goals, and right before my eyes, they all came to fruition in quick succession. Then suddenly, he was gone and was living his lifelong dream. The man stayed in touch and I continued to see him intermittently over the course of the following years.

Each time we crossed paths, a new man stood before me. Modified through the process of being loving towards himself, following his life's passion, and consistently working towards living to his best version, I was, and continue to be, astounded by the transformation.

A dragon character emerged in my work: Drakon. He was at first a solitary creature, and then over time was joined by new dragons and a raven, Ravyness, to reflect how life lessons and feelings surrounding these life changes played out into the larger scope. A shift in the narrative emerged; the dragons became mentors to Ravyness through life examples of living authentically to one's joy.

This deck also employs the use of love language to assist in promoting an authentic connection to the world; the timepiece (time), a heart shaped locket (gifts), a key (acts of service), Divine Tree Goddesses (affirmations), and ghostly forms (touch). These symbolic meanings are intended to help tarot readers to look beyond the classical interpretations and consider what life actions can be worked upon to help one move towards their best version through the use of love language.

I hope you will enjoy the journey with Drakon and Ravyness.

I first began exploring the concept for this deck as a reflection on the life action plan I had developed, put into action, and recorded the resulting effects of. At times the shifts from one way of being to the next were indeed painful and challenging. I was quick to see exponential results in improving my intrapersonal and interpersonal relationships.

The first foundational step towards personal growth lies in having an open and honest dialogue about one's personality, strengths, weaknesses, and how these aspects influence the situation at hand. By acknowledging how these aspects combine to create the reality before us, we can then address the areas that need to change, if we are ready to change, and create a plan for that change.

The story of Ravyness and Drakon flowed through the cards, connecting their experiences to the essence of each card, and demonstrating how the energy of the card may feel when faced in one's life.

The reversals are seen primarily as alternative positives. It is with an open mindset that the concept of "negative" can be released from the conversation when working with this deck. Oftentimes, when the results require work or are not what we wish to admit and accept, we place an adverse connotation to the event. Sometimes it is a great thing to have things turned upside down, as it is merely how we wish to look at the situation that colors it in our reading.

The reality for Ravyness and Drakon is, though these situations are at times challenging, they are needed for growth to attain their full potential. Thus, even in the darkest moments, there is substantive growth.

The spreads at the back of this book are designed to help with organizing your personal growth journey to become the best version of you.

Embrace. Cherish. Enjoy!

FOOL

"Yes," Ravyness said to Drakon. She grasped Drakon's tail and let him lead the way into the realm of the clouded unknown. His confidence fed Ravyness's resolution that everything was going to be amazing; just hold on tight. And just like that, the journey began.

The Fool card reminds us that at the beginning of every journey, there is a moment when we need to breathe in and take a leap into the unknown, be it by ourselves or with the unexpected dragon that comes along. Simply hang on tight, don't lose your grip, and enjoy the adventure that awaits.

When seen in the reverse, the Fool signifies the feelings associated with stepping into the unknown. This process can be anxiety-ridden as you move to lift the weight of responsibility in order to grow and explore your needs. You will have mentors, friends, and family recognize this need and help push the energy to where you want to go.

MAGICIAN

Ravyness brought together the magical tools. She called out the incantation that had been handed down through generations of ravens. Suddenly, Drakon burst through the chalice portal, full of life and vibrancy. His wings mirrored various paths of opportunities and within them, Ravyness saw herself. Each image that appeared was attainable provided she was willing to do the necessary work and become greater than she had ever thought she could.

The Magician calls on us to acknowledge the necessity of giving time to learn a craft or new skills, to develop new habits, and to embrace efficacy for the future you desire to come to fruition. As you become authentic in these new skills, you change. There may be some people who do not understand this shift in you; give them time to adjust. Those who wish to make this journey with you will admire the growth, while others will drift into the mist of memories.

When this card is presented in reverse, it is time to batten down and learn that new skill and new habits. Decide to dedicate your energy directly to the best use of your time and resources.

HIGH PRIESTESS

Ravyness opened her wings and ascended to the heavens. She formed the foundations from which the Divine stood and from the Divine, Drakon. Drakon spiraled, encircling the Divine while his heart, the essence of a desired sense of being, of love, centered over the Divine's womb. Ravyness sensed the love; the sense of completion was already within her.

The High Priestess calls upon the reader to accept and allow the pull of higher conscious to flow through their senses. It is an acceptance of a higher sense of self, grounded in the essence of the universal love that is needed at this time.

In the reverse position, the reader is found in the role of giving back to those who seek to grow in their lives. They have become the light that others seek, to guide them on to the next aspect of their life journey. It is of the greatest importance that the reader approaches this role in grace and honor. You have the power to shape a future.

EMPRESS

The Empress Drakon carefully assesses with discernment the situation before her. Her wings protectively surround her charges with her tail at the ready to lash out, cutting down the interlopers quietly and effectively without discussion.

The emergence of this card informs the reader to take a moment and carefully assess the situation, opportunity, or person trying to engage their attention. Instinctually, they know what the motives are and what that may mean for those under their care. It is without any hesitation for one with the Empress energy to bring them in or send them on their way succinctly.

The reverse position of this card signifies that at this moment the focus must be upon those that are closest and most vulnerable. The reader is their source of strength and protection. It is time to be everything they need.

EMPEROR

One claw upon the hilt, the other grasping a timepiece, the Raven Emperor has the value of experience and leadership added to his cause. To the west, the sun descends to the mountain range, signifying that throughout his life, he has been an icon of stability, immovable in his views. He is a fixture of continuity, of expectations and rules, time and again.

This card embodies the wisdom of clearly defining expectations and boundaries through time habits developed that are now at the point of efficacy, seamlessly flowing. Others around may consider the energy to be a bit too abrupt, sharp, and callous. However, the reader will find that their lives will flow much smoother as they hold everyone accountable to their rules.

In the reverse key, this card signals for the reader to take a moment and truly reflect upon what frustrates them. Acknowledge what the precursors are to the situation and design a plan of action to modify one's reaction or take steps to be proactive.

HIEROPHANT

Ravyness looked down upon the book, reading the words setting forth the foundations of love, traditions, and compassion to all who crossed her life. While the memory of Drakon rose up as a phoenix in her mind, Ravyness recalled the lessons she had learned so many years before under his guidance. She followed the structure of their traditions and found they gave a sense of stability and security as she grew towards her higher self.

The Hierophant signifies that you need to seek out training to attain the personal growth towards your higher self. Focus upon the lessons that grow your soul, morals, and ethics. These lessons become the backbone and foundation of the experiences that follow: the ones that are held with efficacy.

As this card appears in reverse, you are considered to be the teacher and mentor for others seeking to improve their lives. This charge should not be taken lightly. Be honest with your abilities and refrain from embellishing your skills, as it will be revealed when you least expect it. Be humble, be present, be there for exactly what they need.

LOVERS

Ravyness and Drakon paused and gazed at each other. There was a fundamental chemistry that surprised and delighted them. They shared their dreams and aspirations in the quiet moments of comradery. The love that resonated through their joined passion for the paths that drew them in different ways was sheltered, locked away, from the chaos of the world. Each knew as they grew individually, it made them stronger when together.

The Lovers card signifies that when the right connections come into your life, there is an incredible feeling of kinship and support, and it calls upon one to bring the best version of the self forward. The best version of the self enables a union of common ground which balances out the other and continues to strengthen over time.

When the reverse position appears, it signifies that you have found the calming energy needed in your life. Be it alone or with another, cherish the sense of contentment knowing that the supportive networks that you need are in place and they are there because, very simply, they love you.

CHARIOT

One brought the passion; the other brought the calm. Together, they lead Ravyness through the battles fought on the cerebral grounds, burning away the strands of anger, fear, and anxiety that had imprisoned her mind for too many years, to give way to a life beyond exception.

The Chariot is the champion card of the deck, indicating that there is a support group ready and waiting for you to reach out. It may come in the form of friends, group sessions, or professional services. The past has battled long enough within you; time to make a plan, come to peace of mind, and move ahead successfully.

Reverse position indicates to be ever mindful that others are going to need you to help them, to guide them, and to foster a new mindset which is needed to be successful as the future emerges. Be prepared that there will be times of discomfort that are to be expected as you weather through the storms to reach toward your goals.

STRENGTH

Ravyness and Drakon found that as their energies melded together, they became a force which very few could oppose. Many found the emergence of this new entity to be intimidating as there was expected truth and honesty from all who approached them. True strength came from a place of being open without fear of repercussions.

Strength comes from acknowledging, accepting, and merging the dark and light aspects of the self to create a whole and balanced person. The experiences you have garnered throughout your life now influence how you approach situations and distinguish your boundaries. Your goals are much more attainable as you are no longer running from the truth. You are facing and using that reality to build the self into a confident, successful person.

The reverse of this card indicates that you have two sides of the situation that need to have honest reflection, that need to be given time, and that need to be honored. You may feel torn and battered. Addressing what the underlying concerns are promptly and honestly will give back to you infinitely.

HERMIT

An ancient dragon pulled back the fabric of time and space to allow a slight glimpse of knowledge and awareness to be exposed to Ravyness. The great elder knew the weight of shedding all the knowledge that had molded him throughout his life and suddenly thrusing it upon Ravyness may discourage her from her own journey. He stood ready with the wisdom in moderation she needed to guide her through these solitary moments.

The Hermit reminds one that as the journey may seem alone, isolating, as if the information you want, need, is forever evading you, it is important to stop chasing what you think you don't know. Take a moment and stop. Quiet the mind; you need this time for you.

In the reverse, the wisdom you have gained from your life experiences is now embedded into your entire sense of being. This enables a certain level of forethought when approaching new situations. You are able to discern quickly without much need for engagement or commitment into what is most beneficial. This will help to lead you accordingly with the right mind set for success.

WHEEL OF FORTUNE

The portal was opened. The Divine Goddesses emerged while their essence was still entwined together at the doorway. Each of the Divine represented one the five elements; earth, water, air, fire, and metal. Feeling the energy, the Dragons from the north, east, west, and south were drawn toward the five goddesses. Their energy swirled together creating a chaotic moment of discord, yet, at the portal it was calm within the light.

The Wheel of Fortune calls upon us to set ourselves within the portal, to be the calm within the chaos. Allow others to be as they wish, it is not your business to be involved and is important for you to remain neutral.

The reverse finds us riding right along upon the backs of the dragon, spinning, descending, and twirling at the will of others. Hang on tight, as you have been swept into an adventure and will need an extended time to find a resolution.

JUSTICE

Ravyness pleaded her case to the blinded dragon and the triple goddesses. The dragon listened carefully and asked questions that helped Rayness to further understand the situation. Before rendering justice, the dragon made sure to inquire and listen to all involved parties. It is the dragon's duty to ensure that the sword of truth and the scales of justice remain forever in balance.

The Justice card indicates that now is the time to be absolutely truthful in your desires, words, and actions. It is sometimes difficult to plead what you desire when you may well be saying what others expect, what you have been conditioned to say.

The reverse of this card suggests that your motives for trying to get the universe to side with you were not as pristine as you claimed. It may be time to be ready to be called on your untruths, even the ones that you have told yourself.

SUSPENDED

Ravyness's claws were entangled by the chain of the love locket which hung precariously upon Drakon's talon. A sense of calm enveloped Ravyness as she paused and took in her surroundings. There was a sense that time had stopped. She could do nothing to change the circumstance of her situation. She simply needed to wait out of a pure consideration of love for herself and others.

The Suspended card indicates that although it can be frustrating to not have exactly what you want, when you want it, on your timeline, it is necessary to take this moment and pause. The delay will yield its own rewards in due time.

When in the reverse position, Suspended is the action you should take into consideration, to hold back others from moving forward. You are the chains, you are what is holding everything back. Now one needs to ask, why?

DEATH

Heartbroken, Ravyness cawed out in mourning over the remnants of Drakon. The loss hit her in waves that nearly crippled her emotionally. As each swell crashed and then receded, she found herself able to honor his life in a rhythmic manner. Life initially without Drakon felt jarring, empty, and she felt lost. The light that had inspired much in her life had diminished. Her eyes rose skyward and she realized a new light had emerged—a new life, her own.

Death is not always about a literal death; at times it correlates to a time of being reborn and refashioned in a new path in life. Feeling that you are experiencing a metamorphosis, breath in deeply as the new life takes hold. Embrace and celebrate the release of the old patterns that have long been the constant and move into the life that awaits.

The reverse of this card indicates that there may be resistance on your part, but the change is necessary and essential to your growth. Be mindful that grief over life and love takes varying amounts of time. Breathe in, let it go when you are ready, and live your best life.

TEMPERANCE

Dancing along the chalice's edge, Ravyness moved freely between the realms of spirit and the living. She balanced her needs and the needs of others through love and consideration of time. She was mindful that patience, empathy, and quiet solace were essential to allow magic to grow and develop until it is the right time to come forward into action.

Temperance advises that now is the time to pause and take a step back from rushing to your desires. Reflect upon what fulfills you spiritually and completes you. Recognize you may need to allow for things to develop naturally and fluidly in order for them to come together successfully.

In the reverse, this card signifies that you are being generous in your love in the current situation. You are aware that the path to having the nuances of the concern meld together takes due diligence, patience, and understanding. The desire you wish comes together in a functional manner, a true testament to your generosity, compassion, and commitment.

DEVIL

The Devil bound Ravyness and Drakon to the demands of a materialistic life. Ravyness grasped her locket tightly to remember the freedom that came with love. Both she and Drakon called out against the entrapment, pleading their case for freedom. The Devil would not release his charges from attending to their responsibilities on the earthly plane.

This card signifies for you to be the grounding force at this time. It is not an easy assignment and you will need to be mindful to not impose your will upon others to keep everyone going in the right direction. Be aware that you may hear complaints and cries that you are not being fair; however, you need to be diligent and determined to keep to the plan.

When in reverse, there are feelings that you are merely a puppet being played to someone else's show. You desire to cut the cords and reclaim your autonomy. You will need to work out a plan to address what you need to do in order to gain your power back to you.

TOWER

Ravyness stood over the broken timepiece. She held up her wings to protect the remnants from the approaching storm. The face of the timepiece had masked the love locket held inside. Now broken, Ravyness had to accept the truth of herself: that her gift of time was truly an act of love to those around her. She felt as though the very foundations of her life and all she built had crumbled, just as the timepiece laid in pieces before her. She wondered despondently if she could repair what had shattered when she let it slip from her claw.

The Tower is raw truth. It indicates a moment in our lives when it feels as though all we have worked for has crumbled and has broken apart. Everything that we tried to hide from ourselves and tried to mask from conscious thought lays before us, undeniable. It makes us face our secrets. Once it is exposed and accepted for what it is, we can then rebuild a future, stronger than before.

The reverse of the Tower indicates this is a moment that, although you have met an adverse situation, you are able to quickly assess if it is needed for you to leave or stay. However you choose, you are able to quickly pick up the pieces, reassemble, and develop a new game plan to continue along your journey.

STAR

Ravyness perched upon the edge of the chalice to look up at the bearer of the second chalice. A fragment of Drakon's reflection played upon the liquid surface. He poured out his dreams, hopes, and desires to her under the wishing star and cast them to the tidal currents to form and meld with the events that would bring them to fruition.

It is so easy to make wishes and put one's desires out into the universe. It is quite another to be willing to work toward these goals. Dreams typically do not materialize on their own. They take a commitment to move from general desire to a driven passion to make them into a reality. Otherwise, your desires will wash away into the mass of empty wishes made by so many before you. Consider which desires you are willing to focus upon, and develop goals and plans to make them into reality.

The reverse indicates that you have the gift of listening to the wishes, goals, and aspirations from others without biases. You are able to inspire others to develop what they need to give themselves the best opportunity for success. You are able to ebb and flow with the changing currents with ease.

MOON

Ravyness kept her head held high, looking to the heavens, and away from the scene below. She no longer desired to be the savior. Drakon had flown too close and broken the surface. The ocean caught him in the torrential current of emotions controlled by the Goddess Divine.

The Moon card signifies that you have the power of choice. You can choose to give in to the drama and emotional chaos of the moment, or raise your head high, look to where you truly wish to be, and work your way there. Your life is not bound by the emotions and choices of others, but only by how you chose to act.

In the reverse, you are the controlling waters. Your words and actions have the power to heal or harm. This power comes with great responsibility and accountability. Be mindful to ensure the direction you push the situation in is that which improves lives.

SUN

Time felt as though it stood still as Ravyness and Drakon held a sacred gaze. They saw their true selves mirrored in each other's eyes, reflecting a profound connection that traveled to new levels of understanding, love, and joy. Independently, they led their own lives and created their own happiness. Together, their joy grew more radiant as the days and years passed.

The Sun card suggests that you know how to create your own happiness. You inspire others with the confidence to take action and accountability of their own lives. As these accomplishments come together, be sure to celebrate and honor the successes found in others and yourself.

In the reverse, the Sun signifies that you need to work on understanding what brings joy, success, and happiness into your life. It is not upon others to create love and bliss for you. You are the one responsible for how you perceive the moments that are then celebrated.

JUDGMENT

The energy of the dragons transformed. Their spiritual selves rose from the caskets with arms reaching towards Ravyness, seeking compassion, acceptance, and resolution. Ravyness granted them the peace they sought. She led their souls through the night, readying them for their next journey as ancestral messengers and guides for those who remained among the living.

Judgment signifies that you have reached a point in which you need to find a mentor, a guide to help you with the transitions that occur during major life events. You need to have compassion from those around you as you accept your role in the current situation, move to resolve the past, and lay it to rest.

The reverse of this card indicates that what you have been trying to forget and avoid is the past. The faster you fly from it, the more it will continue to creep into your consciousness and effect your current relationships with yourself and others. Now is the time to address the events with a trusted mentor, guide, or counselor. You need to have peace and happiness in your life.

WORLD

Through the chaos of the universe, Ravyness and Drakon strove to find a way to reunite their worlds. In each meeting, they found that they had each grown in confidence, purpose, and appreciation. They continued to improve their personal lives, and brought inspiration to live to the best versions of themselves.

The World reminds us that everything is going to come together in the most amazing and supportive of manners. As you develop a clear purpose in what you desire to attain, it becomes easier to form a successful plan. Take time and write down exactly what you want to change in your life or what purpose you wish to work toward. Our dreams and goals do not simply happen because we wished them, but because we are willing to put in the work to give them best chance of success. This card indicates that you have the energy required to follow through with your desires, which then grows your confidence.

When the reversal appears, things will still come together in a general sense. The responsibilities that you have toward others will feel overwhelming at times. Be sure to give into your dreams and continue to work at them, albeit slower than what you would have liked. However, success and growth are there.

ACE OF CUPS

Time and the locket were chained together for an eternity at the base of the chalice while the protective arms of the Goddesses guided Ravyness toward her higher spiritual self. Drakon watched from a distance, awed at the transformation, and felt compassion knowing it was time for Ravyness to test the waters and fulfill her sense of self.

At the beginning of any journey, there needs to be a moment that you are willing to give yourself the time and love to achieve the best version of yourself. Taking a moment to begin the process to identify your weaknesses and strengths is needed during this time. Always remember that you have significant support all around!

The reverse of this card reminds you that by giving yourself emotionally to all causes, you may not have enough to refill your own needs. Step back and breathe, and make time to honor yourself.

TWO OF CUPS

Breaking from the heart of Drakon, Ravyness and the Goddess emerged. The Goddess reached upward toward the moon while Ravyness spiraled around Drakon. Their forms intertwined in a dynamic balance of love and spiritual connection. Just as the sun and moon adorned the chalices giving balance to the light and dark aspects, Ravyness and Drakon cherished and supported each through their personal spiritual fulfillment.

The foundation of your emotional health is based in love from those who support, cherish, and love you. These significant people are active pillars in your life, and on the hard days they are there to lift you up and bring you back into the light. They find a way to weave a balance of closeness and supporting your independent nature to explore your emotions.

The reverse of this card indicates that your goals have a very grounded, healing nature, and they are able to pull those you love along seamlessly. Choose to be the light that others need during these moments.

THREE OF CUPS

Drakon and Ravyness savored a brief moment to honor friendship, happiness, and personal milestones. They toasted to their continued well-being and told of their personal successes and triumphs. Then, with a knowing look to one another, they took flight to continue their journey.

The appearance of this card indicates the enjoyment of the moment of emotional wellbeing, and celebrating the connections and foundations made with those who support your successes, both small and big. This moment serves to be just a brief meeting of kindred spirits as time permits.

The reversal signifies that you are wise to keep your support network small. Allow them to know the goal and steps you are planning. Once they know, they are able to help keep the momentum toward a new emotional health.

FOUR OF CUPS

Ravyness patiently perched within the shadows cast by the cups, each in its own manner fulfilling her spiritually. She cast her gaze to the sky, dreaming of the passion and fire to ignite her soul. Ravyness practiced the wisdom to wait for an emotionally healthy situation to come into her life naturally.

Learn to find what spiritually fills your cups and brings personal happiness. You may desire to have additional relationships to complement your life. Take time to ensure that the ones you allow into your life are going to encourage a functional, spiritually like-minded atmosphere.

In the reversal, take the time to establish what you want to bring into your life emotionally. Be clear, be specific, and know it is perfectly fine to keep to oneself and wait for exactly what is emotionally the right fit for you to move in that direction.

FIVE OF CUPS

Drakon placed a protective wing over his face. The truths poured out of the cups and burned away the membrane, for there was no escaping the reality of his feelings, and his controlled world began to tear apart. He was so caught up in the moment of exposure, he paid no heed to the cups that he was able to keep from spilling over and the spirits that watched over him.

Denying the truth is certainly not helping your situation. Accept what it is, be accountable. You are able to keep all of the additional truths you are not ready to face carefully in check.

The reverse signifies that you are drowning in the emotions that are overflowing into your life. They have caused you to pull away and shield yourself from those who love you. Take down your guard, it is time to address and face the feelings to be able to move on.

SIX OF CUPS

Drakon and Ravyness shared lighthearted and humorous stories of their lives. Aspects of their personal happiness came to the surface easily and fluidly. Together they celebrated their successes and offered insights to grow and move their lives to new levels of achievement.

This card indicates a collaborative and supportive atmosphere is found with those who are most significant to you. Be sure to listen closely to ideas given and contribute back to the conversation as your experiences and ideas may well lead others to new journeys they had never considered.

When reversed, pay attention to the flow of conversation. Should you notice the conversation is consistently being started and maintained by one in particular, then be sure that balance is brought back into the relationship or explore and ask why. It may be time to have an honest conversation.

SEVEN OF CUPS

Ravyness looked onto the visceral surface in the cup. The locket appeared, opened, and showed the truth of Ravyness's deepest desires: to be held in Drakon's embrace for eternity.

Wishes and dreams are the essence of this card. Be aware that opening yourself up to what you desire requires honesty and a willingness to be heartbroken. These are simply desires that have yet to have a grounded plan formed to assist in building a path toward a successful end. If you truly want what you dream, then it's time to begin to design a plan to give yourself the best opportunity for success. Sadly, you will need to remember, you cannot affect another's free will of choice.

In the reverse, take a moment and dream the beautiful dream of everything you ever desired. What does your life look like if this were to come together? Are you happy? Is it worth it to work towards? Only you can decide where this dream goes from here.

EIGHT OF CUPS

The Cups have taken precedence, void of symbolism, and overwhelmingly stand in unison with the locket and time at their base. The chain which once connected the pair together long ago, is broken. Drakon, disheartened, flew away into the night.

When this card appears, it signifies that the emotional weight of everything has taken a larger role in your life. There may not be the words to clearly express how you feel as you try to communicate to others to have them understand. It is overwhelming. You may feel there is nothing left to connect with spiritually or emotional, nothing left to mend. Due to the nature of the situation, it is best to leave.

In the reverse, by walking away from the situation does not mean that the situation is going to disappear. It will continue to grow, to fester in the cups until you are ready to address them. Be sure to do so sooner than later.

NINE OF CUPS

A younger Drakon grasped the cup of his dreams. He found it to be emotionally fulfilling within the narrow confines of his environment. Behind him, the cups of his ancestors left behind stood in support of any path or need desired.

You are able to achieve emotional fulfillment in your goals. Look back to generational life lessons and incorporate them as you are moving forward to attaining the best version of yourself.

The reverse position indicates that the emotional trials that you have been moving through are going to push through many levels all at once. This moment may feel overwhelming as so many things are going to come to the surface, making you even more aware of the love and support of those around you.

TEN OF CUPS

Ravyness rose above the cups as the emotional energy of the source flowed out and filled the cups beneath without thought of return. One, however, was left without attention. She knew her limits and accepted that she would do what she could.

Your actions are altruistic in nature. The need to share what you have throughout all aspects of your life is commendable. If you are unable to reach everything, the weight of what you have accomplished far outweighs the few things that were unattainable.

In the reverse, all of the energy from your family, friends, and network are being drawn together to help you when you need it most.

PAGE OF CUPS

The newly hatched baby dragon took in all the sights, scents, and feelings as she looked around her new world. The water intrigued the baby. She watched the ebb and flow of the torrential currents, captivating her imagination.

You may find yourself lost in the currents of your subconscious mind, making it difficult to focus on the larger concerns. Allow for the flow to work through your mind. There is a message there, but only if you allow yourself the freedom to be fluid and to see the situation with new lenses.

When this card appears in the reverse, you have broken through your shell that protected you for a very long time. Your heart is opened to build new relationships and give yourself an honest opportunity for happiness.

KNIGHT OF CUPS

Perched upon the edge of the cup, Ravyness became her own Knight in shining armor. Armed with compassion, empathy, and spiritual health, she took a gracious sip from the cup and flew to meet her destiny and offer aid to those along the way.

When this knight appears, it indicates that you are your best complement. You have the power of a positive mindset that encourages healthy relationships for yourself and others. These are quick in nature, but the effects are long lasting.

The reverse of this card signifies that you need to find a mentor to guide you to better understand your personal value and shift the narrative within your mind.

QUEEN OF CUPS

Lost in a world of her own, she stared at the liquid surface that reflected the swinging pendulum motion of the broken timepiece behind her. Her attention held captive by the fragmented image seen for a brief moment, disappearing, and then back, time and again. She was oblivious to the chaos of the ocean waters that crashed upon the cliffs and the encroaching tide.

This Queen lives in a world of her own mind, engrossed in searching for what was once there; her realm is in the past. Rarely does she wish to be of the present to address concerns that are ever growing and surrounding her situation. Be sure to pull your gaze upwards and see the reality of your situation.

The reverse of this card indicates that you have time to delve into the moments that have led you to now. Explore the nuances and reactions from others to gain a better understanding of your role and how it has effected your current circumstances.

KING OF CUPS

Glamorous and fully aware of his splendor, Drakon wore his feelings outwardly. His responses and actions were dictated by how he felt at that moment when counsel was sought. The answers received today versus tomorrow would depend upon what had developed between the two time periods. He functioned within the realm of his feelings as they occurred. This King was not highly known to have empathy towards another's plight.

If you need to make a decision on your current situation, understand that it is based upon how you feel in this very moment. Your sense of self and what is going to bring you the greatest joy is essential when this card is drawn. Put yourself first, your happiness depends upon being honest with those around you by establishing a boundary.

When in the reverse, this card suggests that your feelings may alter from one moment to the next as new information appears. Acknowledge your feelings and continue to grow into what makes you happiest quietly, and refrain from overly vocalizing at this time.

ACE OF SWORDS

Perched upon Drakon's tail, Ravyness verbalized her desires and dreams. Once the words were spoken, they extended to the realm of the air and to the universe. The universe had a rather mysterious way of beginning to lay out the opportunities to have desires come to fruition, provided Ravyness was willing to move forward and complete the work necessary.

The foundations of change begin by bringing your thoughts into open communication. Verbalize what you truly want with clarity. The clearer you present your desires, the more easily an action plan can begin to be formed, and your intentions have a way to manifest into reality.

The reverse of this card indicates others may need you to listen to their ideas completely before jumping to a plan. Be sure to give space and be present as they disclose their deeper desires and as they make their plan to move to their higher self. They want you to be a part of that journey.

TWO OF SWORDS

Ravyness precariously balanced two swords upon her beak. Her attention was focused solely on the perceived tasks and conversations at hand, which left her unaware of Drakon's plight.

Be cautious when you take on unclear tasks that are open ended and require your complete attention or in which the communications have a leaning towards prejudices. Through unintentional neglect, relationships that matter most will simply float away.

In the reverse, allow yourself to feel out the current situations even though you don't know all the particular details. It focuses your energies and allows you to rise above those who would distract you.

THREE OF SWORDS

In a few honest and revealing words, Ravyness realized the secure world she had lovingly constructed was falling away around her. She had not been ready to hear another's truth, that which broke her sense of stability and love.

Truth has a harsh way of piercing through one's heart. The pain and feelings that the self is falling apart is normal. Through this exposure and acceptance of reality it enables you to leave unhealthy situations, take time to grieve, and allows you to heal to be ready for greater opportunities and happiness.

When this card appears in the reverse, a damaged heart can take a long time to heal. Be sure to talk about the root of the grief and allow yourself the time needed to bring peace to your life.

FOUR OF SWORDS

Ravyness closed her eyes, enjoyed a moment of secure quiet. She was unaware of the fiery dragon approaching from the mountains, and only too late would she hear the war cry.

Be mindful of the consequences of dropping your guard at this time, as others may be waiting to catch you in a state of being uninformed and ill prepared when they come storming in with their agenda.

The reverse of this card can indicate that the people with whom you have discussed the actions that need to be done have got your back, so you can take that much needed mental health break. No worries, they can handle whatever comes at them during your absence.

FIVE OF SWORDS

The damage was done. With the swords still embedded in his wings, Drakon gave a guttural scream, filling the crimson sky as he realized the cost of his actions, his words. Ravyness took up the remnants, the truths, and could now see how everything had been connected, layered, and now exposed.

You have a choice. When communications and actions break down, others may seem to have the upper hand, but do they? You are still standing, still intact. Use this newfound knowledge as a life lesson to push forward to a better place and continue to follow your passions.

In the reverse, you have said your piece. Time to move on and not to return to this situation. There is nothing left to be repaired.

SIX OF SWORDS

Ravyness landed upon the boat, sailing to new horizons and experiences, leaving the life that had caused strife and misunderstanding in the hands of those who dwell in those realms. Ravyness neglected to notice that the turbulent clouds were growing across the skies.

When you know a fight is no longer worth the battle, it is time to pack up and leave. Your energy and passions are better focused elsewhere, be it career, love, or community.

When in reverse, it is wise to remember that wherever you go, the past does not simply go away. It follows you like a cloud, a fog that keeps you from living fully. Be sure to wrap up matters so they do not flow into your new life.

SEVEN OF SWORDS

Ravyness heard a noise in the sky and looked up. Drakon flew overhead, clutching swords from questionable origins. A few of them slipped from his grasp and came falling down upon Ravyness, adding a momentary terror in her quiet day as she dodged them succinctly.

You may feel you have full control of the situation and know all the nuances of communications, however there are some critical conversations that have evaded your awareness until by chance you catch a few pertinent details that come your way.

The reverse of this card indicates that new information will be arriving soon. Be sure to listen closely to what is being said; it is highly doubtful that it will be repeated a second time.

EIGHT OF SWORDS

Blindfolded, Ravyness listened carefully and felt her way through her surroundings. As the wind whistled past, each of the Swords made a distinct sound, almost as if they had an opinion on the current circumstances based upon their own biases. She listened intently, but knew ultimately, her direction was her own.

People are full of what they think you should be doing based upon their lenses. Be mindful to allow them the space to speak their minds but know that anything in regard to your life is absolutely up to you.

The reverse signifies that you will want to take time and listen to what others are saying. Each carry a grain of truth that will help you make a decision in regard to your next action.

NINE OF SWORDS

Ravyness had ignored the fiery dragon from earlier in her journey. Now he manifested fully in her subconscious throughout the night as she attempted to slumber. He brought to life her inner fears, and demons rose to play in her mind relentlessly.

This card indicates that the thoughts that weave through your mind are just that, thoughts. When light has been shed upon the situation, it lessens its strength. Be sure to talk to the people involved about your concerns and allow them to do the same so that all parties can move on to better and healthier situations.

In the reverse, you have been sounding the alarms and feel as though you are being ignored. Time to up the game and go to the next level to have your concerns addressed.

TEN OF SWORDS

Ravyness knew it was not the time to voice her feelings. She had considered the greater needs of Drakon's destiny and desires, and refrained from giving weight to the concerns of the heart that been building inside her. She knew her time and love were bound in another world and wisely kept such knowledge from Drakon.

Responsibility and dedication come at a price. They do not permit one to simply walk away; you have said you would take on these projects. You need to give them the time that they deserve to be successful.

The reverse indicates that you will need to be understanding of others in what they have chosen to have as their priorities. It has nothing to do with you, do not take it personally. This is their journey for them to achieve the best version of themselves. Be proud of them and wish them well.

PAGE OF SWORDS

A youthful dragon took in her surroundings. She was aware of even the smallest of movements. She broke through the serene, smooth surface of the frozen lake and realized immediately her effect upon the world: it would be earth shattering.

Be aware that you have the energy to say very little, but the results are felt immediately. Give yourself a breath and make sure that you really mean what you have said, as people are going to base their response on what you present.

The reverse indicates that with a bit more wiggle, you can break the cycle of being stuck in the same conversation which never seems to have a resolution. Now is the time to push a bit more to bring the conversation to a conclusion.

KNIGHT OF SWORDS

When the Knight of Swords appeared, she was ready to upset the balance in Ravyness's life, but did so from a place of love. She realized that the current dynamics were not working and addressed it succinctly.

When working with this energy, consider why you feel you need to say something or take action. Is it from a place of love or a place of fear? Fear places an unhealthy filter on the relationship that is not relevant to the situation. Be mindful that you are not projecting your fears upon another. When our actions come from a place of love, it is only to see a person grow and develop into their best version of themselves. Speaking from a place of love can be difficult for others to hear, but it is necessary to have people speak the truth when we need it the most.

When in the reverse, be ready for others to be open and utterly honest of the changes they would like made to improve the concern at hand. Be sure to hear the concerns fully and be present before acting.

QUEEN OF SWORDS

The Queen's penetrating eyes stared directly at her quandary. She had little tolerance for insolence and trite behavior, had impeccable control of her verbal spars, and kept a tally of rights and wrongs of those who crossed her path. She was not an entity that anyone should ever consider showing less-than-class-act etiquette.

The energy of this Queen is a force very few know exactly how to respond to. It calls upon you to hold you and everyone to the highest ethical and moral standard. Either they meet it, or they don't. You are not bound to give others a second chance, as you don't have time or the energy to waste upon those who are disrespectful to the rules.

The reverse of this signifies that you need to work with this energy from others in your life. Be prepared that you are going to be receiving the cold, honest truth. Hold yourself to the highest standard possible or face the consequences.

KING OF SWORDS

The King of Swords was a formidable energy to engage in any project. He presented a calm, cool, and calculating attitude. One would be wise to tread with sensible caution with this King, as he says exactly what is on his mind without foresight to the long term consequences.

This card indicates that now is the time to be direct and to the point with exactly what you want and who you want in your life. Just know that the actions taken now will have long term effects that you will need to contend with at a later time.

In the reverse, be prepared to stand your ground when others attempt to push into your world without invitation. Your words are able to cut right to the point effectively.

ACE OF WANDS

Ravyness burst through the clouded veil, ready to take action toward her intentions under the fiery sun resting in the autumn sky. She knew her passions and had built the confidence in the power of her voice to make them happen.

The creative voice is a formidable energy. It captures the imagination, encourages one to explore new avenues, and builds an ongoing anticipation of new experiences. Allow this energy to be the inspiration for moving forward with your dreams and passions.

The reverse of this card indicates writing down your desire, creating a plan of action, and allowing yourself to fall into your dreams completely and utterly.

TWO OF WANDS

Ravyness and Drakon discussed matters of where their life passions were calling them. Drakon picked up his wand, readying for flight to explore the world that resided beyond the mountains. Ravyness stayed within her world to develop and grow her creative passions.

To stay or to go, that is the question presented in this card. Know that as you make your plans, they are your plans. Do not expect others to follow your passions, nor should you follow their journey. You need to allow for yourself to grow in your own way and vice versa.

The reverse signifies that your actions are truly done with the intention of love for yourself and others. You are the grounded force that others look to when components of their life feel off-kilter. Listen and be mindful of their long term goals for their happiness when discussing this; it is about them, not you.

THREE OF WANDS

Ravyness and Drakon took time to share their adventures, projects, and latest passions that continued to transform them towards their best version of themselves. The meeting was brief. The ideas generated were considerate and appreciated, as they had the creative vice to bring about greater happiness within their personal lives.

Be sure to reconnect with those who know what your passions and dreams are as you are working towards them. Share ideas and heed advice given: it is done so with a type of love that only desires to see you become the best person you can possibly be and build your own sense of happiness.

In the reverse, be ready to take to heart the ideas that others share with you and act on them immediately. These ideas and experiences will reinvigorate your passions on your journey.

FOUR OF WANDS

The wands connected one to the other in perfect balance and harmony. Ravyness celebrated, as balance had been achieved through the dedicated work towards a common passion with Drakon.

There are times that you need to have the help of others to reach your goal. Everyone has a role to play, and without them meeting their deadlines, you cannot meet yours. Be sure that you are reaching out to the right people to bring your project to success.

In the reverse, you are able to take these tasks under your wings and bring things together with little assistance from others.

FIVE OF WANDS

The White Ravyness valued her time and love that she brought to all components of her life. Fellow ravens offered up their ideas freely of what they felt was the next best move for White Ravyness to consider. Knowing her mind and her heart, she knew exactly where her passions were leading her and kindly humored the suggestions for a moment more before moving along.

People are going to tell you exactly what they think you should be doing. Be mindful to refrain from overly engaging or defending your position. Simply thank them for their input and carry on.

The reverse signifies that, indeed, you need to pay heed to what others are saying especially as it has a common thread of concern. Sit and listen to their concerns, they are aware of a developing pattern that needs to be addressed.

SIX OF WANDS

Drakon raised Ravyness in a celebratory moment, as a pivotal step in the journey had been achieved. They enjoyed the moment and within the next breath,they were quietly back to working toward their next goal.

Achieving one's goals requires dedication through difficult times; the layers you need to cut through are so ingrained from childhood that you must unlearn the old habits, develop new patterns, and maintain the new way of living. Those who are a part of the journey are going to notice these changes in you and celebrate them.

In the reverse, you have made significant changes in breaking from past dysfunctional behaviors. Take a moment and get used to how the new you feels within the environment you find yourself. Is it supportive? Has it changed as you have changed?

SEVEN OF WANDS

Ravyness knew her boundaries. She had no trouble in defining them and holding her ground. She was flanked on her sides by a pair of Divine Goddesses, supporting her decision that she had the right to keep certain paths in her life to herself.

There are some paths that you may not feel comfortable allowing others to share with you, and it is perfectly okay to tell them no. This life is your own and you are under no obligation to disclose every nuance to others.

The reverse indicates that you should absolutely not disclose your ideas and plans. If in the business realm, secure copyrights and trademarks before releasing your project ideas.

EIGHT OF WANDS

Ravyness flew within the chaos of the wands. Finding her cadence and rhythm within the moment, each wand that came to be in her grasp led to a new idea which then crossed the next wand. As she moved through the wands, her experience and expertise grew.

This is a time which things feel literally up in the air and unsettled. Step back, and as each idea presents itself, take a moment and grab hold of it. Work with the idea, then as the next comes along, allow the last task to drop away and attend to the latest. You will find that by knowing your time to work with each is limited, you will be making swift work.

The reverse of this requires that you move deftly between ideas. Assess their relevancy to your life and be willing to discard the weak links effectively.

NINE OF WANDS

Only when Ravyness realized that projects had consumed her entire life, did she turn her attention back to what had always been her constant: to see her beloved timepiece had been broken irreparably. The time she had relied upon to always be there, was now gone.

Be mindful of the time commitments various projects require you to make, as they inevitably will pull you away from moments that have an even greater meaning long-term and from those you who love you. Time will never return, you are given one opportunity. Do you really wish to miss these moments?

In reverse, the swift pause happened for a reason. You will still meet your deadlines. Take a moment and see to the relationships that have suffered due to the focus you have placed upon your creative vices.

TEN OF WANDS

Ravyness accepted her responsibilities with care and graciousness. She carefully held her wings to the sides to assist in the precarious act of balancing all of her responsibilities. All of her focus remained upon them, leaving no time for frivolity or folly.

The current situation requires that you dedicate yourself to the responsibilities that have landed squarely upon you. This is time to take care of everything that you have already obligated yourself toward and refrain from taking on any additional tasks. Be clear and concise that you have hit your maximum: others will understand.

The reverse of this card means it is time to shed some of these responsibilities. You have taken on too much and others are more than capable of helping you through these moments. You need to allow them to help.

PAGE OF WANDS

Grasping her wand, the little Ravyness walked in a determined fashion knowing exactly who she was and the power she wielded. Her impulsive energy knew only the adoration of the universe for her ideas and actions. Under the protective watch of Drakon and the Divine, they worked together to ensure that nothing comes to hinder this Page's creative vice.

There is a very unique energy associated with this Page. This particular card indicates that wherever you place your energy, your goal and desires are met with the mindset of "it is thought, it must be so." Once you feel the power of this new process of thinking, others will fall into place without question.

The reverse of this card indicates that before you step forward with that delicious idea that arrived at the best moment, please take a moment to disclose what you are considering. Listen to a respected mentor, elders, or your inner voice and consider the potential consequences before proceeding.

KNIGHT OF WANDS

Sensuously, the Knight of Wands seamlessly seduces the mind and brings those who cross her path to reawaken their passions. She calls forth the joy, the love, and the sensual side once lost to bubble up and run rampant through veins and right into the very breath of existence.

When within the care of this energy, it will feel as though you have had a resurgence of your passionate side brought back up effortlessly. It is noticed by others around you as they respond in kind, which continues to build and grow your passion for your project. Now is the time to bring together the people who are essential to bringing your plans to fruition in the final stages.

The reverse indicates that there is a person about to enter your life, or already present, that has the ability to bring about the deepest desires to emerge as easy as it is to breathe. Cherish this person. They are not destined to be in your life for long.

QUEEN OF WANDS

She rose through the fires like a Phoenix, this Queen ignited the passions of anything she came into contact with, and burned away the inane to have it rebuilt instantly and greater than what had ever been perceived before. She was a persistent force, unwilling to accept anything less than the best the world had to offer.

You have expectations of yourself and others to attain the very best version of the self and to follow passions. Stay true to this course. Those unable to handle this level of drive from you will simply take themselves out of your realm.

The reverse of this card indicates that you know the fire is within you. It can help you or it can consume you. It is wise to simply reach out to a kindred spirit to have assistance before you burn within the situation you created.

KING OF WANDS

Driven to dive directly into what invigorated his very essence, this King was one to take on things in fiery wild passions that would make a lesser Drakon hide. He had no time for those who were unable to meet him in every aspect fully and utterly in the present.

You need to have people in your life that are living in the present, in their own light and passions. The energy you carry is one which renders others to stand and admire your ability to have things miraculously come together. They may not understand that it is due to your diligence and passion to your cause that your reality is created.

In the reverse, this energy has a tendency to set in the nature of the impassioned workaholic. Your ideas and passions have consumed you at all levels. It is best for you to work through this energy as fast as possible.

ACE OF PENTACLES

Ravyness perched above the doorway to all the possibilities that can and do exist as she journeyed through life. Her dreams, her voice, and her passions are all valid and have value in the world she has created. She knows by bringing together all she has learned throughout her life, she has the skills needed to accomplish anything she desires.

You have now arrived at the moment that requires that you have faith in the fruition of all that you have worked toward. From the humble moments of moving through your emotions to bring about healthy relationships, learning the power of your voice and ideas, and using the creative passion that resides within you to place together the nuances of a plan, this card indicates that it is time to put all these components into action.

The reverse of this card: though you may not believe you are ready, you are. Have faith that the journey before you is most assuredly going to have moments in which you want to go back to the old habit; don't. Keep moving forward. You must move forward. It is the only way to go.

TWO OF PENTACLES

Drakon slid smoothly between two sources of abundance. He was utterly committed to these two fruitions as they were exactly what he had dreamt, strived, and worked towards for many years of his life. Due to his focus on the projects, Ravyness, left to her own devices, built a life for herself and flew away to follow her passions, wealth, and adventures over the mountains and onto distant lands.

This is a moment that you find what you have diligently worked toward through this journey is now the main focus of your life. This brings clarity in your vision as to how you need to keep the wheels in balance and prosper seamlessly.

The reverse of this card is one of recognition that others have their goals and projects that are imperative to their sense of success. It is not for you to judge them for the commitment of time their lives require right now, but reflect on what needs to happen in your life to bring you joy.

THREE OF PENTACLES

Ravyness studied the plans that were laid out before her. She looked over to see how her plans had been progressing with the help of a new friend, who recognized the benefits of working together to have the project come together through comradery.

It is important to review your plan often to ensure that you are staying on task and making your deadlines for completion. Be sure to share your plan with people who are going to work with you to ensure that it comes together.

In the reverse, there are going to be people walking into and out of your life that are willing to play minor roles, and will help you to complete the smaller aspects of your plans. Ask around and people will know of the perfect ones to help you.

FOUR OF PENTACLES

Ravyness found herself rationing out her financial responsibilities impeccably. She was aware of every nuance in her budget of time and resources as it related to her survival and growth. Due to her diligence in building financial stability, Drakon sailed through her world utterly unnoticed.

The moment has come to put yourself and your needs as a priority over other fun and adventurous interests that cascade all around you. Remaining focused is a challenge as the slightest movement to daydream of fun times can shift the balance in such a way that the careful balance will be gone immediately.

The reverse of this card indicates that you are so focused upon the day-to-day balance that you are forgetting an important component: yourself. Take a moment and step away from the workload you have taken on. You need to do so as a way to reenergize yourself and to show love to yourself.

FIVE OF PENTACLES

The Divine Tree Goddess was cut down. The mentor that Ravyness had come to regard as her grounding force was gone. The world was beginning to make less and less sense. Ravyness cawed at the remnants and at her locket to dispel the secrets. She was so engrossed in searching for a way to break open the secret that she never realized it was Drakon who encompassed the pentacles and held the locket's key.

The stable spiritual structure which had been relied upon for so long has been removed unceremoniously. There are new supports growing in their place, however it is rarely the same. You have a plethora of questions in regard to the secrets of life that have yet to be released to you. You will need to adjust how and with whom you discuss what you want in your life. Look to unconventional sources to help.

The reverse of this card indicates that you are to face this moment on your own. You have life lessons associated with secrets that you have locked away and it is time to address them.

SIX OF PENTACLES

Ravyness and Drakon understood the power of gifting and affirmation as a form of love language. By giving this type of love language, they developed an ebb and flow of positive actions that were met by more inspiring actions. Each one brought about a happier relationship between the unlikely pair.

Giving meaningful forms of affection and kindness has powerful concussive results. You set the tone for positive interactions in your relationships across the board. This simple yet powerful shift in mindset yields bountiful results.

The reverse of this card can indicate that as you give to others, your actions are not being met with reciprocation or appreciation. If you find yourself giving to others consistently and they are not meeting you in some sense of the middle, then please, reevaluate why you feel compelled to give when you are not receiving.

SEVEN OF PENTACLES

Ravyness perched upon the porch adornment. She moved with it as the breeze swayed the tokens, causing them to spin in place, never touching one another. The bright pink evening sky with the surreal clouds caused her to pause as she took in the scene that encompassed her, seeing it as if for the first time.

As this card comes into a reading it suggests that you need to take time to evaluate what you think you know and what you have accomplished. Consider how you feel about the work you have put forward at this point: does the return on your investment match what you had dreamt? Be honest. If you are unhappy with the answer, then it is time to find your way between the guidelines that can sometimes feel like a trap, and allow yourself to fly away.

The reverse of this card suggests that you are the keeper of your domain. You have worked diligently to have these components come together over the course of many years. You should certainly take a moment and appreciate all your hard work.

EIGHT OF PENTACLES

Ravyness raised her eyes from her craft to look up to the potential abundance that danced upon the string's end, waiting. Once she finished her work, she reached up to take a token offered for her services and then she went on to her next piece.

Your work is recognized and there are people who are willing to pay for your services. Be sure that the work follows your passion, and to charge the amount that you need to truly honor you and your skills. This also indicates to be open when people appreciate your skills and you are valued.

The reverse of this card indicates that you may simply create an incredible product, ideas, or to bring beauty to the world without asking for financial compensation. You need to be paid for your work, otherwise there may come a time where resentment will build and you may feel compelled to walk away from what you truly love.

NINE OF PENTACLES

Ravyness and Drakon gazed at one another as the Divine elements danced upon Drakon's wings. They had stayed by each other throughout the journey of living their personal and professional lives and bore witness to the growth taken to bring about their best version of themselves.

In the upright, this card indicates that your life has fallen right into place. Your goals and objectives in your life action plan have come together and now is a moment to sit in quiet contemplation to reflect on the nuances of what has been accomplished. Be sure to share with those who have been steadily supporting you and your vision.

The reverse suggests that you have made incredible progress with the help of others. Be sure to give them credit for their role to bring your dreams to fruition.

TEN OF PENTACLES

Ravyness and Dragon danced upon the winds together before they flew back to their realms and back to their dreams. Together they brought a shared joy to each other's lives and cherished the moment.

Taking moments from the drive that has encompassed your life, to enjoy the bounty you have accomplished with those who have supported you through the emotional growth, realizing the power of your voice, and the creative vices that have developed your sense of happiness is what is needed at this time.

In the reverse, be sure that you are connecting to those who know your journey. Tell them, they are your support network that will always be there to lift you up and remind you of all the progress you have made.

PAGE OF PENTACLES

This Page knew that all her expectations would be brought to fruition. All that she desired came together through the course of a season. From the time the seed of dream was cast to the maturation of desire, many found it hard to believe that such abundance was achievable.

There is an effervescent energy that surrounds you. You have the ability to make things grow out of nothing, to flourish, and succeed with as much ease as a summer day. The excitement you bring everyone simply wants to bring it together immediately.

The reverse signifies that all of the aspects of the current happenings are intertwined and directly related to your actions. You have sown the seeds and they have grown beautifully, and are almost ready to harvest.

KNIGHT OF PENTACLES

This Knight was very much the dreamer who just momentarily set his feet to the ground, gazed towards his future, and saw what was coming next in his life. He held his dreams delicately and with love. Knowing that his aspirations and what he wished to bring to reality were essential to his happiness, he was certain to strive to find partners that built upon this nature. He was not a dragon to settle with one for long, as his dreams would forever overtake him and lead him to follow the wealth of exploring new wonders and possibilities.

When you receive this energy from this knight in shining amour, it promotes the power of giving to yourself to achieve your aspirations and desires. You can certainly inspire and share in the love, but ultimately it is the focus of the destiny that you desire.

The reverse indicates that you are looking back to the success that has brought you to where you find yourself at this moment. Much like the Hermit reflecting on the lessons learned, this Knight considers the successful patterns that have emerged over the past year. Utilize these lessons to set up the next phase of your plans.

QUEEN OF PENTACLES

Queen Drakoness fully controlled her wealth and abundance. She drove a very high level of expectations for herself and the world. She invited those who entered her realm to be exceptional and strive to be their best selves, above reproach.

You are at the helm, in full control of your every dream, and your every action. This energy calls you to meet every challenge and excel beyond expectation. As you accomplish this, you see abundance come to fruition over and over.

The reverse indicates that you are tied to your abundance and wealth completely. You simply cannot step away, and to think that you would want to would be erroneous. You absolutely love your life.

KING OF PENTACLES

The King Raven took in his realm. He was generous, warm-hearted, and transparent in his actions. He worked hard to create a stable world. His resources enabled an abundant life for exactly what he needed and what he could provide to others in his life. He appreciated the finer things in life and welcomed those who maintained a positive mindset towards success and personal growth.

As this card appears, it is a crescendo of the life journey that you have worked hard to create and the sacrifices made along the way. You have established a stable world that, with minimal oversight, continues to produce the life that provides all that you need.

The reverse of this card indicates that you have created your empire on your own accord, and you carved your own river from which your abundance flows. The abundance has taken many incredible forms in your life: love, career, friends, and so much more. Be sure to recognize your blessings.

THE REALITY OF PERSONALITY

This spread explores the nuances of personality as it affects the situation and helps to build a sense of self-awareness. This process is challenging and requires one to be ready for an open and honest dialog with the self. During this reading, it is important to keep in mind that throughout this book, the positive aspects of reversals, cards with images drawn to be upside down, have been explored.

As you begin this spread, take a moment to reflect upon you. Who are you? How do you handle situations that you find challenging? Shuffle the cards thoroughly.

This spread in completed in three parts.

1. Lay the first three cards in a vertical manner. These cards represent the three main components of one's personality that affect the area of concern.

2. Then, lay cards on both sides of the first three cards in the order shown. Begin by placing card 4 to the left of card 1, and place card 5 to the right of card 1. Continue for each of the two remaining personality influences.

3. The cards to the left (cards 4, 6, and 8) represent the "pro" aspect of your personality in the situation. The cards to the right (cards 5, 7, and 9) represent the "con" aspect of your personality in the situation.

THE ART OF CHANGE

The Art of Change spread explores how tarot can be used to create an action plan to promote change and growth.

Begin by writing down your goal on a piece of paper or in a journal. Be sure that it is something that will be kept and viewed often. Each step will need to be attainable for you. Determine the timeline you would like to see this goal accomplished.

Now, focus upon that goal, shuffle the deck and select three cards in any manner you desire.

FLIPPING OVER CARD 1:
Consider what action is going on in this card.
What action does this card suggest
that may help you work toward your goal?
When do you want to have this action/objective completed?

FLIPPING OVER CARD 2:
Consider what action is going on in this card.
What action does this card suggest
that may help you work toward your goal?
When do you want to have this action/objective completed?

FLIPPING OVER CARD 3:
Consider what action is going on in this card.
What action does this card suggest
that may help you work toward your goal?
When do you want to have this action/objective completed?

CONCLUSION

The journey to become the best version of you takes time and commitment. This deck was developed to begin the process of opening the door to having an honest dialog with the self. This level of honesty with the self can be uncomfortable and painful as the fabric of what has always been comfortable stretches to fit into the new skin, the new reality that has become you.

I hope that this deck has opened a new perspective on how Tarot can help in your life journey to become the best version of yourself. Be willing to allow people who want to support you to be there, in their own way, without expectations.

Thank you for opening your life to this deck and to the change that can happen.

ABOUT THE ARTIST

Beth began her Tarot journey during her formative years of college when her mother presented her sister with a Tarot deck. Intrigued by the images and symbols therein, Beth spent the following decade studying Tarot and how the symbols interacted to create a deeper understanding of the self.

In 2006, Beth began to design her first Tarot deck, the *Theban Tarot*. Her work was followed by one watchful Tarot collector, who encouraged her to continue and then prompted her to print her work.

Through the years, Beth explored Tarot as a means to capture the experience of living. Often disguised through humor, the layers to her images offer an unabashed level of honesty for one to meditate upon and develop oneself.

Beth has now 100 decks that include a mix of Major Arcana, Tarot, Lenormand, and Oracles. Her mass produced works to date include: *Tarot Leaves*, *Dream Raven Tarot*, *Bleu Cat Tarot*, *Guardian Tarot*, and *Tarot at the Crossroads* (written by Shannon MacLeod), all available through Schiffer Publishing/Red Feather.

Beth's work can be found by visiting www.bethseilonen.com.

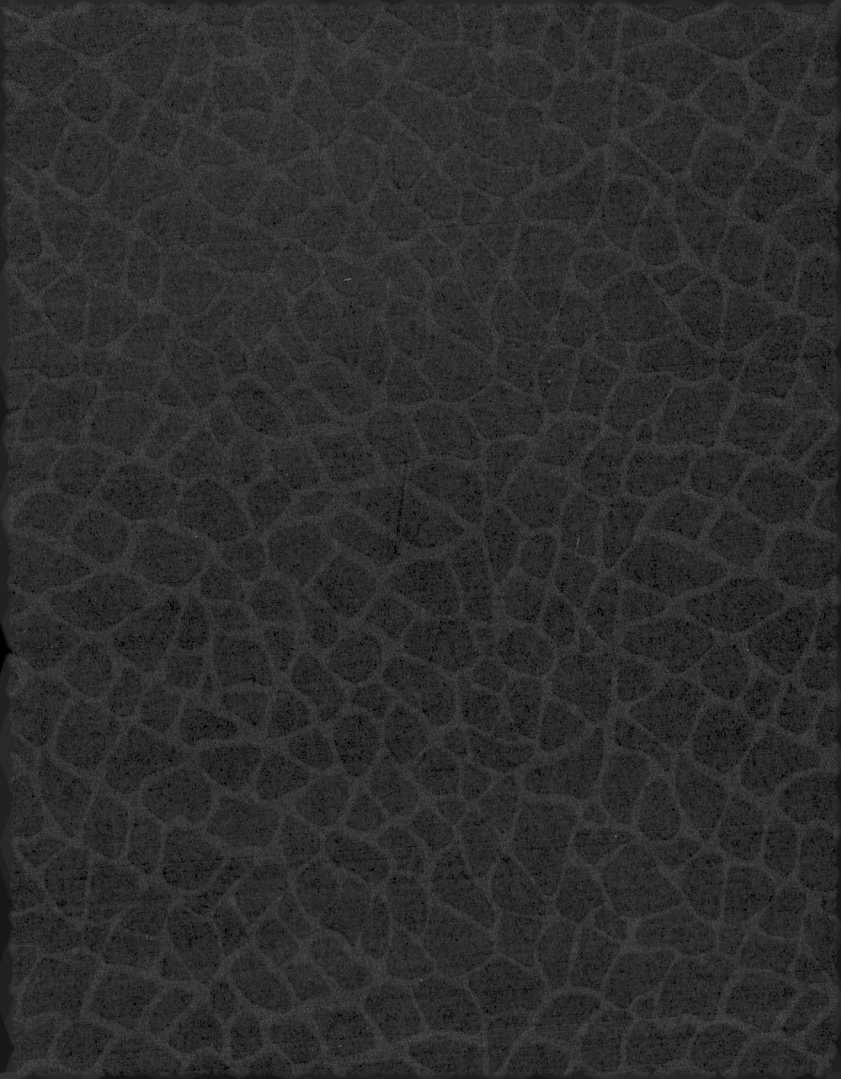